THE

PACIFIC

NORTHWEST

POETRY

SERIES

M000265775

LINDA BIERDS / GENERAL EDITOR

FOR THE CENTURY'S END

POEMS: 1990–1999

JOHN HAINES

UNIVERSITY OF WASHINGTON PRESS

SEATTLE & LONDON

For the Century's End, the first volume
in the Pacific Northwest Poetry Series,
is published with the generous support of
Cynthia Lovelace Sears.

Library of Congress Cataloging-in-Publication Data
Haines, John Meade, 1924–
    For the century's end : poems, 1990–1999 / John
Haines.
        p. cm. — (The Pacific Northwest Poetry series)
    ISBN 0-295-98145-8 (paper: alk. paper)
    ISBN 0-295-98160-1 (cloth: alk. paper)
        I. Title. II. Series.
    PS3558.A33 F67   2001
    811'.54—DC21   2001033189

The paper used in this publication is acid free and
recycled from 10 percent post-consumer and at least
50 percent pre-consumer waste. It meets the mini-
mum requirements of American National Standard
for Information Sciences—Permanence of Paper
for Printed Library Materials, ANSI z39–48–1984.

For Hayden Carruth, Poet and Friend

CONTENTS

III

IV

V

PREFACE

The political content prominent in some of
the poems collected here has been for me inevit-
able, an element not to be refused. Events in the
daily news, articles and photographs in various
journals—the wars and devastations, the endless
flight of refugees—any one of these may at times
suggest a theme or require a response. How one
chooses to deal with this is a matter of individual
talent and persuasion. I have always sought a
poetry that, as in the classical past and in the
case of many of our prominent modernists, can
include the public events of our time and do so
in a way that makes them at once contemporary
and unavoidably linked with humanity's long
and troubled history.

By their nature, some of these poems have
exacted a long period of growth as ideas and
themes have suggested themselves and been
renewed. I refer here especially to three of the
longer sequences, each of them dating initially
from the early 1970s. "In the Cave at Lone Tree
Meadow" resulted from my exploration of the
ancient Chumash Indian culture of southern
California, and the artifacts that remain of that
culture in museums and books, but also in the
many petroglyph sites and painted caves to be
found throughout the region. Lone Tree Meadow
is but one of these that I was able to explore at the
time, but one of a special significance for me.

"In the House of Wax" began with a visit to
the Royal Wax Museum in Victoria, BC, in the

summer of 1974. One or two later visits to similar
museums in Seattle and San Francisco added
to my impressions, but the sequence of poems
was slow to clarify as I sought to add to the many
historical figures and events suggested by those
waxen images. A few of the poems meant to
complete the sequence remain unfinished.

"A Guide to the Four-Chambered Heart"
originated with a drawing I made for one of my
step-children, in which I depicted a human
heart pierced by an arrow and divided into four
sections, or chambers, in each of which I placed
a symbolic figure. The individual sections of
the poem grew slowly from that moment.

On occasion, prompted perhaps by a news
article, I have been moved to include in my
poems something of the contemporary attention
to the exploration of "outer space," and our
attempts to find some new ground in the solar
system—the meaning and possible consequence
of these efforts. Whatever the success of indi-
vidual poems, I continue to feel that a poetry of
our time should attempt this. Two of the poems
included here, "Star Photo" and "NEAR Travels
Far to Find Eros," have been for me particularly
important in this respect.

I have often felt that we write at our best, most
deeply and permanently, out of an ancient and
durable sense of our earthly life and experience;
that our everyday lives and events may at times
return us to an older mythological source, even
when, as may be the case, we are not aware of
this. I could not, for example, have written "The
Legend" as it stands had I not lived the life I did
in my early years in the wilderness of Alaska; and

then, many years later, in my initial reading of the epic of *Gilgamesh*, reflecting on the forest life of animals and the role of the hunter, recognized a parallel, an instinctive return to a very old human conflict, one that has its spiritual dimension not to be put aside.

Again, in "The Telling," in the main voice of the poem and in the fortune-teller's quoted words: for reasons not immediately clear, certain events in our lives may at moments take on a dimension beyond the ordinary. A few words spoken, a passage in a letter, a gesture—perhaps a sequence of these—seem to speak for something we had not guessed the meaning of. It is important here that the subject or event connects us with some-thing intuitively deeper in the self of the author or witness, and is not merely seized upon and exploited for a momentary success. To create, in a work of art, a piece of writing—a poem, a novel, a drama—something of a modern mythos, remains the essential task.

Inevitably, as one moves into one's later years, and with the publication of a collected poems, one considers what may be a last book—a sum-mation, or perhaps a postscript. On that note, I make no special claims for the poems collected here, other than to say that they represent, in their form and substance, much of the best I have written in the past decade. In a future book I hope to add to and amplify what is here, as the claims of the writing, of coping with the time of one's life and with events in the outside world, continue to assert their presence.

JOHN HAINES

ACKNOWLEDGMENTS

I would like first of all to thank Linda Bierds, Pat Soden, Gretchen Van Meter, and others at the University of Washington Press, for helping to make this book possible. It has been a pleasure to work with them during the past year.

I wish also to thank the editors of the following publications in which many of the poems in this book first appeared: *Alea*; *Amicus Journal*; *Artful Dodge*; *The Atlantic Monthly*; *Black Moon*; *Doubletake*; *The Hudson Review*; *Manoa*; *Many Mountains Moving*; *Mystic River Review*; *The New Criterion*; *New Virginia Review*; *The Ohio Review*; *Pemmican*.

"In the House of Wax," nos. I, II, III, VI, first appeared in *The Sewanee Review*. "City of Orphans" and "Politics and the Dead" were first published in *The Sewanee Review*, vol. 108, no. 4, Fall 2000.

The following poems were published in *Temenos Academy Review*, London, UK, in 1998: "City of Orphans," "Eclipse," "The Legend," "In the Cave at Lone Tree Meadow."

"The American Dream" was first published in *The Sewanee Review*, vol. 109, no. 3, Summer 2001, and in *Metre, An American Special Issue*, Belfast, Ireland, 2000.

"A Guide to the Four-Chambered Heart," with illustrations by Joy Haines, was first published by Larkspur Press, Monterey, Kentucky, 1996.

"The Last Election" was published in *The Best American Poems of 1999*, edited by Robert Bly.

FOR THE CENTURY'S END

POEMS: 1990–1999

Poem for the End of the Century

I am the dreamer who remains
when all the dreams are gone,
scattered by the millennial winds
and sacked by the roadside.

The solar clockhand stopped,
confusion and fury on the street
—so much idle paper
shredded and tossed aside.

The small, dim shops of the tourist
trade are shuttered and locked . . .
Nightfall, and the buyer turns away.

One more stolen fortune spent,
another century gone
with its fits and desolations—
I leave my house to the creditor wind.

Tell me if you know my name,
whose face I wear, whose stored-up
anger fades to a tentative smile.

I am the one who touches fire,
who rakes the leaves to watch them burn,
and who says once more to himself
on this calm evening of earth:

Awake! The stars are out,
mist is on the water,
and tomorrow the sun will return.

I

The Legend

I understand the story of Gilgamesh,
of Enkidu, who called the wind by name,
who drank at the pool of silence,
kneeling in the sunburnt shallows
with all four-footed creatures.

I know the name of that exile,
the form that it takes within us:
the parting and breaking of things,
the distance and anguish.

I know too, in its utter strangeness,
that whoever asks of the sun its rising,
of the night its moonstruck depths,
stirs the envy of God in his lofty cabin.

And when Enkidu awoke, called
from his changed, companionless sleep
—singly, in glittering pairs,
the beasts vanished from the spring.

The forest bond is broken,
and the tongued leaves no longer
speak for the dumb soul lost
in the wilderness of his own flesh.

Leopard, gazelle, insect and floating
leaf—all that had life for him:
the moon with her wandering children,
the storm-horse and the shepherd-bird,
become as salt to his outspread hand.

Let him go forth, to try the roads,
become that wasted pilgrim, familiar
with dust, dry chirps and whispers;
to die many times—die as a man dies,
seeing death in the life of things.

And then descend, deep into rootland
—not as a temple-gardener, planting
with laurel the graves of gods and heroes,
but as one grieving and lost . . .

To ask of the dead, of their fallen
web-faces, the spider's truth,
the rove-beetle's code of conduct.

By such knowledge is he cured,
and lives to face the sun at evening,
marked by the redness of clay,
the whiteness of ash on his body.

III

By stealth, by the mastery of names,
and one resounding axe-blow
rung on the cedar-post at dawn,
the great, stomping bull of the forest
was slain. Rain only speaks
there now on the pelted leaves.

Overheard through the downpour,
in the stillness of my own
late-learned solace, I understand
through what repeated error
we were driven from Paradise.
The nailed gate and the fiery angel
are true.
            Could we ask them,
speaking their wind-language
of cries, of indecipherable song,
it may be that the swallows
who thread the water at evening
could tell us; or that the sparrows
who flock after rain would write
in the coarse yellow meal
we have strewn at the threshold,
why God gave death to men,
keeping life for himself.

For the strong man driven to question,
and for him who, equally strong,
believes without asking,
sleep follows like a lasting shadow.

In the Cave at Lone Tree Meadow

I

My home is in the rock,
in the fire-thicket, at rest
with fleeting bird shadows.

A pebble fallen to the floor,
the cry of an owl
hunting the stone coverts —
these are my voices.

A little water in a pool
stirred by the wind,
a dry dust bed. I lie awake
and watch the west light
smolder and sink . . .

The sun is almost down.

II

A long time gone, a quiet hunter
carved in this smoky wall
an image of the thing he followed.

Companion or shadow, changing
its shape or its name:
it was fish or reptile, bird,
or something marked like a man.

Made to stand upright, climb
the gritty stone, and overhead
in a ceiling pocked with stars,

be placed among the figures
painted there—beheaded insect,
flying fox—and every track
and feather daubed with clay.

And over it all, the blood-smell
of heat and sun-washed fur
that stands in place of a man,
enters, becomes the man,
and the man falls away like dust.

III

I know that sign, I have seen it
before—the deep, edged print
of nail and pad, a long way north
in the sand at Glacier Crossing.

Thirty summers past, I stopped
by a stunted tree above the creek,
to watch in the thicket below me
the brown, humped shoulders moving,
the great head down . . . and Fear,

like a grass blade trembling,
stood up and turned toward me
its face, ferocious and blind.

I followed where he crashed and fled,
as if it was myself I tried
to kill, seeking a blood-splash,
a message bitten in a tree,
a grass-bed crushed and reeking.

The summer burned away, and far
into the mist and frost
that followed I tracked him,
hunting still the cold benches
for a pelt sunned on the ice
in a leaf-fallen country.

I find my quarry here,
in the sand of an old sea-bed,
uplifted and changed to stone.

IV

I have lived a long time,
followed the stone track of things,
the snail-trace and watermark
of our troubled passage.

Have seen in the mirrors
and windows, my own or another's
—in the clay masks of men,
images that were not true,
though once I believed them.

Out of such waste and deception
I climbed my own steepness,
my way forgotten, slept
in the red cave of my heart.

An old companion came to me,
roused from his matted sleep,
divided in his nature, and
thick with our quarreling blood.

V

Hoarse and wounded, his indrawn breath
and blind face looking down:
man-headed beast or beast-headed man,
pulled upright from the same clay—
a paw divided into hand
or closed in a hoof, treading
the marshes, fixed in eternal snow.

Whisper of names, fever of old mythologies,
stale causes and coupling priests.
Who made fire and who made shadow,
the blood move and the flesh walk?

Was it dream or actual man I saw?
A forehead puckered with thought,
a wind-truth that furrowed the grass—
no more than a shrugged mattress
that loomed and seemed to speak.

I ask once more in this late hour
where nothing is forgotten
and nothing forgiven, but now
as in the first light of a first dawn,
this one clear face in the darkness.

And like a slow, damaged figure of sleep
he left me, parting dry leaves,
a step in the great silence beyond.

VI

The red sand burns a deeper red,
night and this cave are one house.

I wait for a sound I know —
the slow, climbing tread
that has followed me all my life
and will track me down.

I will be eaten by him in my sleep,
his stone feet forcing me down . . .

Until I am dust and scattered,
my bones dry as dust, on the floor
of a cave in this mountain.

Star Photo

You are here, in this country
of diminishing returns,
on this patient rock
slowly cooling in a cloud.

This is your country,
the only one you can claim;
yet it is no country,
no land, but an eddy of dust
in the holocaustal wind.

Think of a city growing distant
in the night below you—
the bridgelights winking, traffic
no more than a fiery ribbon,
as the aircraft lifts
away and the clouds close in.

Now *earth* is only a name, and
the galaxies, fused and glittering,
are more than a name—the sum
of discarded theories,
realms of terror and perplexity.

And the woodland you learned
to love has vanished—
no trees bent to the wind,
nothing but the memory of trees,
sand, and pulverized glass.

You are here, on this stretched
and icy field, open range
without limit, with no horizon,
no imaginable hedgerow;
no view but a flickering whiteness
at the edge of deepest darkness.

You are here because there is
nowhere else for you to be,
and you cannot leave without
taking everything with you . . .

Shepherd and eternal sentry,
the cloud-horses you ride at will,
stars for your sheep,
and a comet for a watchdog.

The Ancestors

And from the marshland across the water
came suddenly a cry, repeated,
as a great flock of birds,
or of creatures that looked like birds,

rose from the cypress, clapping
unfeathered wings, their sawbills
shearing bark and leaves . . .

Wheeling, gathering height and numbers,
they turned toward us, crying
with voices like no birds
we ever knew, piercing and shrill.

And in one interval of that monstrous
crying we felt another sound,
as of ponderous feet treading
the marsh, and thickets crashing.

Then saw above those distant trees
huge heads and sinewy necks
upthrust, as though that forest
were waking, root, branch and crown.

The light darkened overhead,
the nightwind rose . . .

And now with those towering beasts
and the ever-gathering flock,
the marsh and the waters were moving.

NEAR *Travels Far to Find Eros*

Sent into Space on a three-year journey
—gone now, never perhaps to be seen
again, never again to be welcomed,
to be touched and questioned.

What will we think of to say to those
still waiting, still searching the skies,
when the allotted years are up,
and NEAR is still far from its meeting;
Eros wandering alone in its orbit,
or crashed in that glittering company?

A year spent probing the stellar dust
for a secret buried underfoot in
the forest soil or fastened to a rock
—this broken shell, this stem
of a violet, this wind-blasted tree.

Another year, another comet sighted,
and always this blind human craving,
a search for what was left behind,
a satisfaction no longer to be found.

One more skilled adventure—whatever
it is that fuels the stalled machine
and sends the pilot on his starry quest;

whatever it is they hope to find
out there—an emptiness, a stillborn
terror, but it is not love.

NASA *Dreams Quietly of Mars*

Some day to set foot on the Red Planet,
first to visit, then perhaps to stay.
Quietly, in a prolonged absence, to know
of no other event than such a journey.

To build your city of sand and smoke,
then watch it fall. Listen to the wind
that scours the red plateau; think
of the century's gift that brought you here.

To dream of things a robot cannot do:
play golf with living rocks,
then place at war whatever remains
of your fossil neighbors.

And always in your metal heart remember
that distant home we called Earth,
so quietly sinking in the solar sea.

II

In the House of Wax

I

Far-sighted into yesterday
they stand, gripping
their charters and speeches,
the presidents and kings,
masters of unconscious evil.

Their deputies are here—
judges, robed executioners,
steely and triumphant.

And stunned at their feet,
the beheaded, the betrayed,
healed and hallowed now
in this grave sorrow of wax.

We enter, adjust to the gloom,
to the lighting that plays
on the painted, staring faces.

We think to ourselves, murmur
to the one standing beside us:
"How compellingly strange
these people are, and yet familiar
to the world we left behind us,
the street and the household . . . "

These are the people whose names
we learned, whose lives we studied,
whose thoughts we have become.

Each lighted stage with its play
of the lost and the violent—
comedians and stuntmen,
heroes transfixed in purpose.

We pause, to read once more,
in deliberate, bald summation,
what art, wax, and history
have made of the dead:

something more than a mirror,
less than a telling likeness;
an ideality slick with blood.

How easily in the live heat
of truth and summer
these actors wilt and perish.

Henry of Church and England
is here, savage and senile,
still laced in his armor;
his lopped and stunted wives
stand grouped around him.

Bismarck in his iron corset,
endlessly dividing Europe;
Wilhelm, that strutting dwarf,
abject in abdication.

And here, the fatal mischief
of Sarajevo—how swift a fire,
how long a burning, came
of the Archduke's festive ride,
his shot and bloodied tunic.

And no more telling prophecy
in the wake of armistice
than that one dated cartoon
with its hooded sentry
and its graveyard owl:
"It has been six years . . ."

How easily a puff of smoke,
a square of burnt cloth,
a shocked cry, can change
the world, and leave it
neither worse nor better.

IV

Here is a man, thief or martyr,
hanged at Damascus Gate
with a hook through his gut.

He swung, seared by the sun
and kissed by the night.
And maybe one of the market
women brought him water,
and maybe not—once seen
by the Sultan's watch,
she might have lost her hands.

As in the time of Richelieu,
certain men the crown accused
were exposed in iron baskets
like plucked birds.

They fouled their nests,
starved and blackened until
they died; and the city lived
with their cries, their rank
mortality, night and day.

The hook is black and crescent,
the body swings, inert,
as if asleep and dreaming.

The guidebook tells us the man
survived his hook and lived;
it doesn't say how long.

V

Here, with his tins and furs,
is Minuit, buying Manhattan.
We see the Dutchman's flourish,
the Indians' foolish feathers.

He takes their land, and they
his bitter gifts, his brass
and trinkets—so little cash
in place of an earthly kingdom.

Wolfe, Montcalm, on the plain
below Quebec: the one dying,
the other condemned to follow.

We pass, reading from face to face,
from book to book, uneasy
that among these celebrations
so many rigged transactions
have gone unquestioned.

And all our wigged colonials,
our Franklins, conspiring
with their strongbox keys
and profitable lightning—

that so much ink and dust
and shuffled paper conceals
their tidy pilferings,
their purity and blunted wrath.

Were there rooms in this house,
each with its tabled motions
and false partitions
might furnish a history,
one slow truth at a time.

But never in our late arrival
have we stilled confusion,
to learn how great a folly
follows in the wake of fathers.

From their deliberate violence
we come to our own lamed
misrule, its slick banality
and crime without passion.

To Ike, to Kennedy and Ford,
golfers and temporizers;
to perennial candidate Nixon,
whose cheek was never turned.

Out of his sleek arrest
he steps toward us,
as if to greet a voter —

a fixed, ferocious smile
on the blue jowls
brushed with powder.

VI

Nothing we have painted
and framed in our passage—
neither prayer nor courtship,
nor solace of sleep
and self—escaped the grip
of these iron centuries.

Here, in a row of lighted
cases, a few artifacts
are on display. No comfort
to us now in that familiar,
edged interrogation . . .

But the biting persuasion
of chains and collars,
of inching racks, fire tongs
and screws—in the eyes
of kings and churchmen
the instruments of truth.

And whosoever might trespass,
on whatever lawful ground,
would find for his solace
a more forbidding marriage.

As once in a stone embrasure
I saw a belt for virgins,
a hinged and rusted clasp,
with a lock, and a slit
for functions—all but one.

Imagine with what shocked
dismay a man might grope
for his sweetness there,
and all too soon awaken,
clamped in his ecstasy.

VII

Another room,
with smaller people
and thinner walls.

Here the Queen plays
with cryptic cards,
hands out assignments:

"You are the Hunchback,"
she says, "and You
the Hangman, and You
the Jack of Trades."

She pares and quarters
her venomous apple,
calls for her mirror,
and her image smiles
to watch her glass
fill up with poison.

Beauty is sleeping,
the Prince is awake,
and far in the forest
a frostlight winks
from the Sugar House.

The Witch is singing
and lighting her oven.
The Woodcutter's
wayward children watch,
they break and nibble
the sweetened glass.

The images whisper
and darken, conspiring
in their tumbled tale
of fretful spinners,
of drones and dumble-
dores, wise eggs
that speak and shatter.

And it looks as if
the painted sleepers
in this dreamworks
are about to awaken:

the crafty Queen
and her players,
the musical mice,
the drones
and the spinners—

All in a scampering
rush, to find
the nearest exit . . .

As the looking glass
draws us deeper
into the bright play
of shadows that melt
and run and freeze . . .

The mad, mad romp
of children, of rabbits
and dwarfs, who keep
their strange hilarity
in so much horror.

VIII

Call those from underneath,
the sold and trodden,
their slow and sweating sons,
elevate and crown them.

Patch up their clothing
and wash their skins,
rub their faces
until they glow,
and their dull eyes brighten.

Give them speeches to learn,
and eloquent gestures,
power to grasp,
laws to break and mend.

Great heat and furious labor
bring on in them
this drear and mystical change:

At first a swinish fattening,
and then a leaner look,
and in their eyes
the same feral glitter
of their late unkindly masters.

They sicken as they flourish,

until like wickless candles
they slump and totter;
their heads are rotten,
their famous flesh
has run to sticky pools.

They die and sleep afoot,
their ignorant hearts
grown wise in the ways of wax.

IX

In all these wax memorials
only appearance changes.

Crowned heads and axes fall,
thugs and jailors rise
and displace each other
in this long, uneasy walk
we have littered
with claims and captions.

The heroes are always welcomed,
are propped and shaven,
their ruddy male composure
is sleeker than ever,
though the great sleeves
and brutal collars
give way to softer buttons.

The paper in official hands
rustles as before,
though it is only paper,
paper in cheap supply,
and not the bleached fell
of a difficult sheep.

And yet the neat persuasions
are seen to tighten,
and each new litigation
is a running noose . . .

All that increases,
all that gluts and fattens,
matures its option here:
Honor to thieves and merchants,
long life to the butcher.

And for the just petitioner—
sweeper of hallways, scapegoat
and discard—no reply
but the rote of legal fictions;

to which he listens, now
as in the days of Pontius,
stricken with understanding.

X

The rooms are large and numerous,
and we in our restless striding
find that they never end.

It is as if we had lived here
always, captive to this endless
and malign instruction;
had served these mighty tempers,
and learned too well
these never-blotted names.

And we live here still,
sharing these murderous spaces,
this blood-haunted silence.

And once we started from sleep,
terrorized and whimpering,
to see in the luminous,
sunken light, the head
of a long-forgotten agent:

a face like a father,
one who might have comforted,
but cannot see or hear us:
bald, vacant, and amused.

XI

All is as it must or might be,
here at the story's end—
the jury dismissed, the witness
excused, and all are guilty.

To have come so far, walked
so easily through so much anguish,
pride, and stupor of evil,
and yet we are standing still,
locked in an echoing foyer.

In so driven, so brief an itinerary,
a day will stand for a decade,
an inch for a mile—so far
has a painted fiction served us.

These bones in their period costumes
would bend if we touched them;
their flesh would yield,
and all the arrangements topple.

But see how they bring toward us
the old, sustaining gestures—
a stride, an arm outstretched—
the furrows in the smiles
deepen, and the red lips smear.

Great captains command, obedient
ranks go down. In all these propped
assemblies I know a substance
neither wax nor wholly flesh—
a tried and mortal nature,
familiar as the warmth in my hand.

XII

Were we not lost, condemned
to repeat these names
and to honor their crimes,
a voice among us might cry out,
speak to those who are
stopped here:
                    Whose faces are these
that melt and run?

Children and guardians, giants
and dwarfs —
                    Oh, people, people . . .
Who are these heroes
and where are their victims?

We who are standing here
with our guidebooks suddenly closed
and all the exits darkened . . .

Until another gallery opens,
or the sun through that skylight
strikes us all —
                    souls in torment,
pilgrims and doting fathers . . .

III

The American Dream

It would have to be something dark,
glazed as in a painting. A corridor
leading back to a forgotten neighborhood
where a ball is bounced from street
to street, and we hear from a far corner
the vendor's cry in a city light.

It would have to be dusk, long after
sunlight has failed. A shrouded figure
at the prow of a ship, staring
and pointing—as if one might see
into that new land still unventured,
and beyond it, coal dust and gaslight,
vapors of an impenetrable distance.

Too many heroes, perhaps: a MacArthur
striding the Philippine shallows; a sports
celebrity smeared with a period color.
A voice in the air: a Roman orator
declaiming to an absentee Forum
the mood of their failing republic.

It would have to be night. No theater
lights, a dated performance shut down.
And in one's fretful mind a ghost
in a rented toga pacing the stage,
reciting to himself a history:

"Here were the elected Elders, chaired
and bewigged. And placed before them
the Charter: they read it aloud,
pass it with reverence from hand to hand.

"Back there in the curtained shadows
the people's chorus waited, shifting
and uncertain; but sometimes among them
a gesture, a murmur of unrest.

"And somewhere here, mislaid, almost
forgotten, the meaning of our play,
its theme and blunted purpose . . . "

City of Orphans

How strange to think of those streets
and vacant lots, the sandhills
where we played and dug our trenches;
the forts we built, the enemies
we conjured to aim our stick-guns at,
and then went home at evening,
to victory, to safety and sleep.

And now the vast acres of rubble,
the pitched and roofless houses,
upended stonework and sunken bridges.
The dog-packs roaming, digging
for the one still-unclaimed victim;
the stray sniper aiming at dusk,
and in the roadside fields,
flowers that explode when picked.

The children wandering from one
burned suburb to another,
seeking that which no longer exists:
a neighborhood, a playing field,
a wading pool or a standing swing;
for a kite to fly, a ball to throw,
or just one pigeon to stone.

And through all this haunted vacancy,
from cellars and pits of sand,
come and go as on a fitful wind
such whispers, taunts and pleadings:
the scolding voices of dead parents,
the lessons of teachers no longer
standing, whose classrooms
are blown to ash and smoky air.

And far-off, unheard beyond the drone
of a single hovering aircraft—
in Paris, Zurich, Prague, or London,
the murmur of convening statesmen.

Kent State, May 1970

Premonitory, her outstretched arms
as she kneels in the spring sunlight,
the cry on her lips that will not
raise the boy lying dead before her.

How often has that image returned,
to fade and reappear, then fade again?
In Rwanda, in Grozny, Oklahoma . . .
Kabul, city of rubble and orphans.

And now the Capitol streets are closing,
an aroused militia at the gates —
the fences scaled by a stray gunman
for an enemy poised ever within.

We are asleep in the blurred ink
of our own newsprint, in the flicker
of our nightline images; in the fraying
voices of distracted candidates.

How long before that prone form rises,
to stand, confused and blinking
on the sunlit campus field; then fall
again in the blood we cannot see . . .

And that long-held cry of hers awakens,
to be heard at last over the stutter
of gunfire — in the glassy echo of a town,
a street, a house no longer there?

Notes on the Capitalist Persuasion

I

"Everything is connected to everything . . ."

So runs the executive saw,
cutting both ways
on the theme of all improvement:
Your string is my string
when I pull it my way.

In my detachment is your dependency.

In your small and backward nation
some minor wealth still beckons—
was it lumber, gas, or only sugar?
Thus by imperial logic,
with carefully aimed negotiation,
my increase is your poverty.

When the mortgage payments falter,
then in fair market exchange
your account is my account,
your savings become my bonus,
your home my house to sell.

In my approval is your dispossession.

11

Often in distress all social bonds
are broken. Your wife may then
be my wife, your children
my dependents — if I want them.

So, too, our intellectual custom:
Your ideas are my ideas
when I choose to take them.
Your book is my book,
your title mine to steal,
your poem mine to publish.

In my acclaim is your remaindering.

Suppose I sit in an oval office:
the public polls are sliding,
and to prove I am still in command
I begin a distant war. Then,
in obedience to reciprocal fate,
by which everything is connected,
my war is your war,
my adventure your misfortune.

As when the dead come home,
and we are still connected,
my truce is your surrender,
my triumph your despair.

Politics and the Dead

Who calls from the paper columns?
Whose voice there in the paragraphs,
in the handbills and leaflets?
Why are you standing so still

in the shadows, unable to speak
your name? Or was it you I saw,
a drifter shrouded in the street,
you lying cold in the doorway.

Your vote cannot be counted now.
Party, affiliation—what are these
to someone for whom the precincts
are deleted, all entries cancelled?

Yet there you are, compromised,
betrayed, hardly a whisper
in the wind of the corridors,
there where the laws are unmade.

Neither citizen nor ancestor.
A rumor of something no longer
required—unwanted stranger
to your own renumbered house.

Blood

Tell me if you see it now,
under your foot, by the roadside—
a pool beneath the public phone,
a stain on the voting-booth curtain.

Someone was here, and someone now
is missing—distracted voices
astray in the thrumming wires.

Tell me if that which reddens
the wind and colors the evening
makes you think of a book—
if the news you read draws blood,
if you feel the wound in your hand.

Turn the pages with that wounded
hand: count the episodes, the raw
displacements gummed together . . .
It is history, now and tomorrow.

A cry that breaks from the crowd
as the speaker slumps and falls;
an image in the theater, a rope,
a sudden flash from the shadows . . .

Something that swells the awnings
like a summer downpour, but it
is not summer, and it is not rain.

The Unemployed,
Disabled, and Insane

after August Sander

He stands alone at the city corner,
an old hat crushed in his hands.
There is no hope in those eyes,
fixed on a scarred and empty street.

On a facing page two blind children
are holding hands. What they are saying
to each other we are not told,
but that they are disabled and insane.

It is 1929. We are waiting for what
we cannot see and have no name for:
a booted stride on a street of glass,
the triumph of a murderous will.

Seventy tormented years have passed.
The refugees are camped at the end
of another road, to cross the border
into that same still-haunted age.

The children there are not yet blind;
they are old enough to see
what this solitary man is looking at,
here at the center of an unturned page.

It Could Happen Again

In memoriam: Hilda Morley

We met in Provincetown two years ago
this summer, companions in the art
we shared, and in our separate lives.
I remember that brief friendship,
and the bond that grew between us.

We walked to the waterfront at evening,
you limping on an injured foot.
And then by the fireside at supper,
in the quiet of that place we liked,
and never once did you stop talking.

I listened: Your life with Stefan,
in the Europe you knew and left behind.
And how you planned to move to London,
to a house you owned in Hampstead,
and finish out your life there alone.

And then you paused, on the one subject
difficult to speak of, so much a part
of what you are and were in our wounded,
distracted world—of refugees and cattle
trains, the forced dispersal of a people.

And you said, quietly but firmly,
in the thoughtful voice of someone who
has known too well what others merely
read, the voice of a gentle seer:
"It could happen again. It could happen here."

The Last Election

Suppose there are no returns,
and the candidates, one
by one, drop off in the polls,
as the voters turn away,
each to his inner persuasion.

The front-runners, the dark horses,
begin to look elsewhere,
and even the President admits
he has nothing new to say;
it is best to be silent now.

No more conventions, no donors,
no more hats in the ring;
no ghost-written speeches,
no promises we always knew
were never meant to be kept.

And something like the truth,
or what we knew by that name—
that for which no corporate
sponsor was ever offered—
takes hold in the public mind.

Each subdued and thoughtful
citizen closes his door, turns
off the news. He opens a book,
speaks quietly to his children,
begins to live once more.

IV

A Guide to the
Four-Chambered Heart

I / THE CHART

Pierced by an arrow aimed toward Paradise,
the heartstem broken from a tree
that stands in perpetual autumn,
its leaves dipped in blood.

A heart like all others, divided in four.
Under the left shoulder a stained
forefinger points to a hidden room
where the dead parent lies,
with a warning ghost at his head.

Here is the place of admonitions.

Below this, a mask in a frame,
a face pulled out of shape,
distorted mirror, and not of one face
but many; their scars and shadows
still mark the wasting years.

Those eyes shrink away as they glance
upon the third chamber . . .

A sunken door, closed many times
by a hand that tugs from within,
or by a wind that blows along the collarbone.
The place of affections may be opened
on a word quietly spoken,
by a hand that knocks without anger.

And last, to the right above, a sun
continually rising, sleeping and smiling,
the light of childhood and easier days.

This heart once shattered by a fault
bobs on a lake of humors,
a bitten apple; or like a swelling plum
shaken on a tree of vessels.

All around are the depths, echoing
as the heart steams and thumps.
And the shaft of the arrow, still wet,
in a wound that never heals.

II / THE WRECK

I came here once, awakened
by voices in my tunnel of sleep;
all inbound traffic stalled,
deflected along strange arteries.

Little at first was clear,
but the strung ribs spanning
deep shadow, the marrowlights
gleaming:
                    Dead End. Stop.

I felt around me the ponderous din
of machinery, a heavy blow
repeated from a hidden source.

Before me the ropes of life
lay tangled and pulsing. I saw
uprooted trees, their stump-ends
stranded in the steaming air.

And on that fatal roadway
were pavement stones upended,
ladders and gaping pits.

Shadowy figures worked there,
blackened and perspiring,
striking their fugitive matches.

With strange beaks and birdlike
shoulders they labored—with groans
and whispers, blurred voices
and grating teeth—heaving into
the ruddy light, rubble
and debris, coins of a dead realm.

I had come to that ancient ground,
the place of no rescue,
where men fight enormous fires
and carry their own dead from houses
they themselves have burned.

As a surgeon might look down
into the open heart he works on:
his gloved hand stopped in its skill
upon the stretched, blood-lighted

tissue, he sees as in a red mist
how his own heart ages and changes,
desire and clear spring
seized to a fountain of rust.

A crossroads where everything crashes;
the towering wrecks never cleared,
but strewn with bitter glass
whose victims bleed but do not die.

Deserted thoroughfare, abandoned
to winking flares, to wraiths of steam
parting in the cold, interior air.

Now only a ghost with a swinging
lantern walks and whistles . . .
A pump that falters and seems to stop.

III / THE FLOWERING PLUM

I planted a stick in the sunlight,
a small red tree wearing
a heart on its many sleeves.

Out of the nursery, thrust down
in the cold soil
of an urban springtime—

I gave it bone meal to grow on,
water out of muddy wells;
I healed its branches,
broken by ice and by wind.

And the young tree sent out roots,
searching under the pavement stone
for a hold on the earth—year
after year, while the nearby houses
filled, or rang like windy shells.

*

Then people grown thick on the land
spoke to each other:

"What is this tree that flashes
in the wind, but gives us
no fruit to eat or to sell?

"Call the man with an axe,
green blood on his blade . . . "

But their children cried out:
"There is joy in this tree,
a warmth in its autumn shade,
and sometimes it sings. Let it be."

*

Continually those red leaves fall,
are swept away in the gutters—
dark pools of blood there,
the shed wealth,
and not of one tree but many.

The morning wind and the evening wind
blow that color east and west,
each ruddy leaf torn loose,
casting its fire in the sunlight.

IV / DEAD LEAVES

My heart is a leaf whirled in a storm,
with many thousands torn
from trees like my own forked solitude.

Leaves, you tangled and seeking voices!
Thousands,
                thousands are on the way . . .

They come behind us, crowding and seeking
—the frail, arrowy leaves,
lobed and dry-toothed, with bitter stems.

Tumbling in drifts, wind-scattered,
over slate, blocking the drains . . .

A few leaves fly to the porches,
they scratch at the sills
with dry and insistent hands:

"What place is this?
                Whose trees and houses?"

Hands like leaves appear at the windows
to point out the way:
                "There, not far,
at the end of the street . . . "

See where the dead leaves are driven,
cast over lots and spiny fields;
there to be raked,
                bundled in carts,
set afire in a smothering heap.

All that was red and pulsing
finds its life burnt in that wind.

Their small, sloping shoulders,
structure of nerves and tendons
collapsed into flame,
                are given as ash
to the sun, lost in a steely mist.

And now cold smoke from sinking bonfires
drifts on the landscape . . .

All memory gone, fiber and root
of my flowering plum stripped bare;
each tree a skeleton standing alone.

Orpheus

She has gone back down the way of blood,
the way of earth and slime,
where the stones are slick,
with nothing but footfalls and echoes,
water trickling in the darkness.
Whatever can be spoken in the hereafter
becomes this silence, this absence.

To carry the dead and the loved,
the lost and bewildered,
through life and death in life,
was your assigned calamity.

To bear one's stricken self for sixty years
is harder still. From looking back,
the heart censures its own conduct,
sees its habitation become
a tilted stone ringed with iron,
and a barking dog at the gate.

Orpheus is dead, his bones a playground
for flies and foraging voles.
Now, in the absence of any singing god,
let that other voice begin:

be it bellow, scream, or roar;
the plain music of crystal breaking,
chirp of frogs, thrash of leaves
in the twilight, mutter of sea-waves . . .

The unrehearsed, deliberate artifice,
older, deeper, and more lasting.

The Telling

"There is one and only one . . . "

So was your fortune told,
as the palm reader scanned
the past, the present
and future, and then went on
in the telling
of an inexplicable journey.

II

I see lines that cross,
that travel together
and seem to part again.

I see a large flock of birds
circling a single figure,
and somewhere nearby,
a small burial is taking place,
with the sound of dirt
hitting a cardboard box.

And once more the lines converge,
are thickened with grieving
and unexplained departures.

I see a forest path; beside it
a waterfall, and someone
diving repeatedly into a pool.

I see a house, divided by many rooms.
Three children are searching

the hallways and opening doors;
they enter a smaller room
and vanish into another country.

I see honor and happiness there.

And you and I were together there,
waking and sleeping, speaking
the names we were given,
" . . . as if we did not know
each other well, but our souls did."

I see how it all combines
and reassembles, completed in this
one unfailing image—a woman
telling fortunes, casting
the future in someone's open palm:

"There is one and only one . . ."

III

The forest path is empty.

That house and its people,
the search and the children's story,
dissolve to an open park
where someone is throwing a ball
at the root of a tree;
others, silent and grouped
at a distance, are keeping score.

And all these characters and scenes
are displaced by shadows
that loom and slowly clear . . .

In that improbable, fantastic place
I shall be planted somewhere
with trees and natural stones,
turned slowly round
in the hollow of obedient earth.

And you, awake in the world,
without a shadow and less
than human, your ghost children
driven before you
down the cobbled mazes —
mouth open,
cropped hair in a fiery light,
and your finally stricken heart,
wondering and amazed . . .

Wounded Life

You, downcast, sitting on your bed,
painting your nails, and saying
to me, "I did this for you . . ."

And I, wondering at your words,
uncomprehending, yet moved
by a silent witness in the room.

I see you now in that very place,
your clothing heaped at random,
your head lowered, reading perhaps
from one of your common books
a story that if one had known how
might have been better told.

Understand that we either grow
or die—die inwardly of that
unlived life we carry within us
like a leaden shadow,
a possibility in thought corrupted.

And of each of us will remain
mostly an image in someone's mind:
a brief light in the summer
darkness, a remembered gesture
like a single unfastened button.

Another Country

Once in a lonely fit
I breathed on your picture . . .

And from its rooms and spaces
took shape this other country
in its own dimension of quiet.

And you in your grief were there,
walking a path by the river
with another and truer name.

You saw a wolf loping before you
on the ice-road, and a raven
that called and spoke to you
as it turned in the wind;

and a great tawny cat raking
the dead wood of a tree,
who looked and did not see you.

And you went on over small hills
of glacial drift and sorted stones,
the season changing as you moved.

The trees you saw were new
to you, yet you called them
by their names: *black spruce,*
white birch, and *alder . . .*

And a small house where you entered,
took from its shelves a book,
and read and slept, and dreamed

that winter came and was long,
lighted by many stars,
and you were not lonely there.

And one spring day the sun
came back, and a sudden weight
slipped from the snow-roof.

And later you sat in the brief
light of summer, bathing,
and making to yourself a song:

Come to me in the shape
of a lynx or a wolf . . .
Come in your frost-fur
on enormous, silent feet . . .

Into that fabulous woodland,
its hunting lairs and icy springs,

For I would follow you there . . .

V

Eclipse

You will speak of our days in whispers
if the twilight wins.

How from our camp on the hill
we saw below us the river whiten,
the town lamps flicker and sink,
and all the traffic muted.

A little wind in the icebound grass,
the clouds parting—
half-shielded in the overcast,
a round face swallowed the sun.

No one came near to tell us
why our shadows faded from the snow,
nor why in that sudden dusk
the chilled flocks, black and strange,
rose up about us—then
settled in the field without a sound.

As once in another country,
at the height of noon,
the summer birds stopped singing
and night came back . . .

So now as then might the year
be ending before the soil was broken,
and summer itself become
a cold sleep inside the sun.

The Ghost Towns

"The North is strewn with cities
of one winter . . ."

I have seen them, the tinderboxes
stacked upon each other,
their wind-structures fallen,
no way to enter now but the gates of frost.

They were lighted by the pressure
lamps of fever, by lamp-men
trimming soot and breaking coal,
reading by the fire of their wicks
the cold logic of the snow.

It was all dream and delirium,
the amazed rumor of gold—a letter
carried in a stampeder's pocket,
unread, and the homeland long forgotten.

As I have held my hand above a candle,
seen the red flesh glow
and the knotted bones darken,

so will these buildings leave
their trusses charred and crossed,
the graveyards lettered
with a script no one can read . . .

And over the bleak and gutted land
no wall to stop the wind—
one space, one frame for all.

Star Struck

I

Wandering blind out of orbit,
in a whispering rush across
the face of our dream planet,

scattering on far fields and
standing towns its silent blaze
of radium, plutonic fire.

II

The impact shattered windows
in our sleep-ridden houses.
We woke too late in our beds,

a people who never before
climbed the enormous hollow of
a tree gone somewhere in smoke.

And under our eyelids, seeds
of light swelled and glittered
in a swarm like yellow flies.

III

Far in space a mine exploded
on a ring of Saturn, set loose
this stone dust of the ages.

And so a starry messenger
fell burning here, stricken
with news of our lives . . .

This earth and its radiant flesh,
born of seawater and sand,
now fused in a violent bubble.

The Ice Child

Cold for so long, unable to speak,
yet your mouth seems framed
on a cry, or a stifled question.

Who placed you here, and left you
to this lonely eternity of ash and ice,
and himself returned to the dust
fields, the church and the temple?

Was it God—the sun-god of the Incas,
the imperial god of the Spaniards?
Or only the priests of that god,
self-elected—voice of the volcano
that speaks once in a hundred years.

And I wonder, with your image before me,
what life might you have lived,
had you lived at all—whose companion,
whose love? To be perhaps no more
than a slave of that earthly master:

a jug of water on your shoulder,
year after stunted year, a bundle
of reeds and corn, kindling
for a fire on whose buried hearth?

There were furies to be fed, then
as now: blood to fatten the sun,
a heart for the lightning to strike.

And now the furies walk the streets,
a swarm in the milling crowd.
They stand to the podium, speak
of their coming ascension . . .

Through all this drift and clamor
you have survived—in this cramped
and haunted effigy, another entry
on the historian's dated page.

Under the weight of this mountain—
once a god, now only restless stone,
we find your interrupted life,
placed here among the trilobites
and shells, so late unearthed.

Roadside Weeds

From Asia, the stony Rift,
from the rank thicket
we have come,
water-borne and wind-carried.

I was once a seed
swollen in a birdcrop,
and you like a tick
traveled in a bale of wool.

We are pest and bounty,
we possess the yard
and claim the field.

Here stands an immigrant
with his heel in the dust,
alien as *black medick*:
great mullein,
lord of the roadside.

Whatever is here is native,
never to be erased
from the chosen ground.

Our roots drink that water,
from the burst pod
a welcoming wind scatters
our seed,

in that field, or this one.

Snow

"In the gloom of whiteness,
In the great silence of snow . . . "

And that is how we remember it:
the flakes falling, drifting
into the noontime city air;
traffic stalled and offices closed,
a people grown suddenly quiet,
polite in their civic attention.

And strange on a following wind
a flock of sea-gulls driven inland,
stranded in the suburb trees,
but alert and quietly waiting,
watching for bread on the snow.

I think of the snow gone black
with coal dust in Ohio, brown
with volcanic silt in Anchorage.
Of the Washington Yard when we
were young, sledding the cobbles
downhill on a quiet Sunday.

And Edward Thomas, from whom
my quoted lines are taken, whose
child saw in the falling snow
the feathers of a white bird
killed on her nest, the shed down
failing in "that dusky brightness."

And now on the lakes and plains
the snow of another age is falling—
that laid-by dream of a continent
stilled in ice and snow, enormous
ghost-herds ploughing the drifts.

And once in Manhattan, when I was
a student, solitary, wandering
the Sunday silence of Wall Street,

a snowstorm that buried the city.

For a Young Student

And there you were, bending over
that heavy book, and I came
into the room on my way to class,
to stop there, looking over
your shoulder, to read the title
and maybe some of the text.

And I saw at the top of the page
the name Flaubert, and the title,
Madame Bovary. You looked up at me,
surprised, almost in fear, when
I asked if you liked the story.
You hesitated, then turned away
and said in a stricken voice:
"Well, it's awfully long . . . "

I thought then of Emma, of Charles
and Rudolphe, the three of them
shut away in that fateful province.
Of her lonely, thwarted passion,
and what it so clearly tells us
of the ungoverned uses of ambition,
that slow poison of an unrealized life.

And I went on to my own class,
to talk of literature, of history
and culture; to speak of character,
of genre, of structure and image—
all the while thinking of you,
of your slow bewilderment, and how
terribly long this life can be.

Days of Slaughter

And so one's dream dies also,
something left by the roadside
as the armored van drives onward.

Another house on another street,
a city stranger than the last—
but still the old life unresolved,
and the stricken heart at nightfall.

To the End

To think to the end of one's life,
think it through and go beyond—
go back to the beginning, to find
one's way into that place where
all was uncertain expectation.

Remember how one sat in a carriage,
rapt and alone, looking at the trees
and the sky . . . the clouds building
overhead, how they moved away
and the sun shone. A light breeze
shifted the leaves and shook the grass.

A voice from the street, a car door
closing, a dog distantly barking.
The sound of a motor running,
and silence closed on the yard,
the street with its numbered houses.

It was all there in that moment,
both distance and welcome, stillness
and departure . . . The clouds moved
in once more, and the sun darkened.

All that remains of a childhood,
restored in a faded album:
the fleeting image of a vacant house,
a dust of snow on the steps—

All that was and would be.

NOTES

I

In the Cave at Lone Tree Meadow (page 10) Lone Tree
Meadow, a remote Chumash Indian pictograph
site in the Sierra Madre Mountains of southern
California.

NEAR Travels Far to Find Eros (page 18) NEAR
(Near Earth Asteroid Rendezvous), the first space-
craft to orbit an asteroid, was launched February
16, 1996, as part of NASA's Discovery Program.
NEAR's year-long orbit of asteroid 433 Eros,
originally scheduled to begin two years after
launch, was delayed until the year 2000.

III

The Unemployed, Disabled, and Insane (page 50)
August Sander (b. 1876, d. 1964) was a German
photographer famous for his photographs of
people in his native Cologne and elsewhere in
Germany. See *August Sander, Photographs of
an Epoch.* Aperture, 1980.

V

The Ice Child (page 75) The poem refers to an article
in *Newsweek* magazine (November 6, 1995) con-
cerned with the discovery by archeologists of the
frozen body of a young Inca woman, 12 to 14 years
of age, preserved in ice at a 500-year-old gravesite
in the high Andes of Peru. The girl, whose face
seemed to speak across the centuries, had appar-
ently been ceremonially sacrificed by Inca priests
to appease the mountain god.

JOHN HAINES is the author of fourteen books
of poetry and five books of essays. His honors
include fellowships from the National Endow-
ment for the Arts, the Guggenheim Memorial
Foundation, and the Academy of American Poets;
the Alaska Governor's Award for Excellence in
the Arts; the Western States Arts Federation Life-
time Achievement Award; the Lenore Marshall/
Nation Award; the Poet's Prize; and the American
Academy of Arts and Letters Award in Literature.
He lives in Missoula, Montana, with his wife, Joy.
Photograph by Peter Iseman, 1991

A NOTE ON THE TYPE

This book was set in Electra, a typeface designed
by William Addison Dwiggins (1880–1956) for the
Mergenthaler Linotype Company and first made
available in 1935.

W. A. Dwiggins was born in Martinsville, Ohio,
and studied art in Chicago. In the late 1920s he
moved to Hingham, Massachusetts, where he built a
solid reputation as a designer of advertisements and
as a calligrapher. He began an association with the
Mergenthaler Linotype Company in 1920 and over
the next twenty-seven years designed a number of
book types including Metro, Electra, and Caledonia.